Scholl, Elizabeth J.

New Jersey.

$29.50

DATE			

FROM SEA to SHINING SEA

NEW JERSEY

ELIZABETH J. SCHOLL

Consultants

MELISSA N. MATUSEVICH, PH.D.
Curriculum and Instruction Specialist
Blacksburg, Virginia

PATRICIA VASILIK, M.S.L.S.
Children's Coordinator
Clifton Public Library
Clifton, New Jersey

CHILDREN'S PRESS®
A DIVISION OF SCHOLASTIC INC.

New York • Toronto • London • Auckland • Sydney • Mexico City
New Delhi • Hong Kong • Danbury, Connecticut

New Jersey is in the northeastern part of the United States. It is bordered by New York, Pennsylvania, Delaware Bay, and the Atlantic Ocean.

The front cover photo shows Long Beach Island in winter.

Editor: Meredith DeSousa
Art Director: Marie O'Neill
Photo Researcher: Marybeth Kavanagh
Design: Robin West, Ox and Company, Inc.
Page 6 map and recipe art: Susan Hunt Yule
All other maps: XNR Productions, Inc.

Library of Congress Cataloging-in-Publication Data

Scholl, Elizabeth.
    New Jersey / Elizabeth Scholl.
        p. cm. -- (From sea to shining sea)
    Includes bibliographical references and index.
    Summary: Introduces this state nicknamed "The Garden State," including its
geography, history, government, famous people and places.
 ISBN 0-516-22321-6
    1. New Jersey--Juvenile literature. [1. New Jersey.]   I. Title. II. Series.
F134.3 .S36 2002
974.9—dc21   2001006983

TABLE of CONTENTS

CHAPTER

INTRODUCING THE GARDEN STATE

This picturesque scene is in Seaville, a community in the southern part of New Jersey.

There are only four states—Hawaii, Connecticut, Delaware, and Rhode Island—smaller than New Jersey. Within its tiny area, however, there is much to discover about this special state.

Named by the British for the English Channel Isle of Jersey, New Jersey is located on the Atlantic Coast, pocketed between its larger neighbors, New York and Pennsylvania. Together, these three states are called the Mid-Atlantic states.

New Jersey's nickname is the Garden State, because it is a major producer of blueberries, cranberries, peaches, tomatoes, and corn. In fact, New Jersey's 9,600 farms produce more than one hundred kinds of fruits and vegetables. Agriculture, or farming, is one of New Jersey's largest industries.

In contrast to its rural farmland, New Jersey also has several major cities, including Newark, Jersey City, and Camden. It is the most densely populated state in the country, meaning that the most people live in the smallest area per square mile. In New Jersey, there are 1,134 people per square mile.

All those people helped make New Jersey what it is today. Many "firsts" took place there. New Jersey hosted the first organized baseball game, the first college football game, and the first professional basketball game in the United States. The first movie was made in New Jersey.

Throughout its history, New Jersey has been home to many famous people, including United States presidents Woodrow Wilson and Grover Cleveland. Modern-day music stars such as singer Whitney Houston and rock-and-roller Bruce Springsteen are also from New Jersey, as well as famous sports hero Shaquille O'Neal.

What comes to mind when you think of New Jersey?

* Inventor Thomas Edison working in his laboratory at Menlo Park
* George Washington and his troops crossing the Delaware River to Trenton during the Revolutionary War
* Stately lighthouses dotting the coastline
* People hiking, camping, and canoeing at the Delaware Water Gap
* Vacationers enjoying summer resorts on the Jersey shore

New Jersey is a small state full of big surprises. You can ski in the mountains, see dolphins swimming off the coast, and collect stones on the sandy beaches. New Jersey is truly a place to be explored.

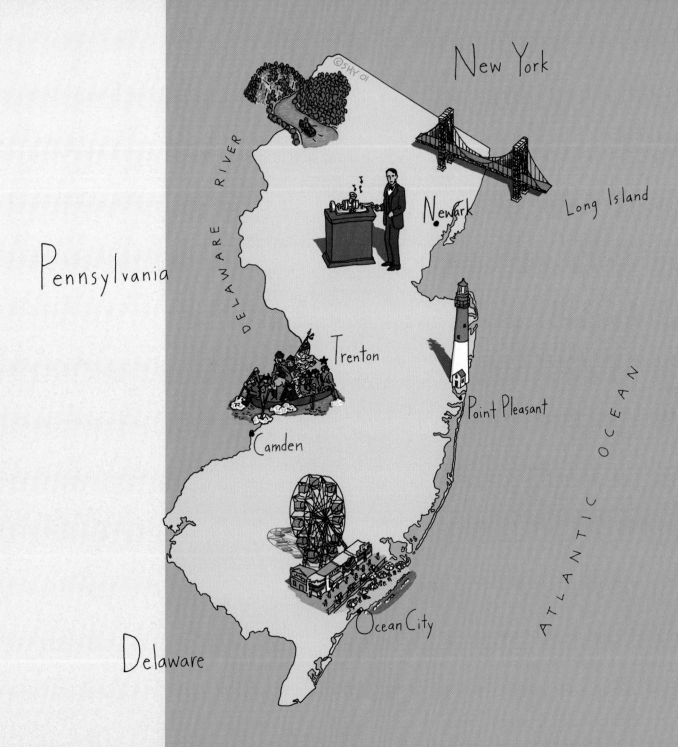

Pennsylvania

New York

DELAWARE RIVER

@SHY_01

Newark

Long Island

Trenton

Camden

Point Pleasant

ATLANTIC OCEAN

Ocean City

Delaware

CHAPTER TWO

THE LAND OF NEW JERSEY

New Jersey is shaped like the letter *S*. The Hudson River and the Atlantic Ocean form New Jersey's eastern border. The Delaware River lines its western border. At the southern end is the Delaware Bay. New Jersey's only land border is on the northeast, with New York.

New Jersey is hard to spot on a map of the United States because it is so tiny. It is the fifth smallest state. Its total area is 8,204 square miles (21,248 square kilometers). If you could drive straight through New Jersey at its longest distance from north to south, it would only take about three hours to drive the length of the state.

What makes New Jersey so fascinating is its diversity. The landscape ranges from mountains to wetlands, and from lakes to farmland. New Jersey has four geographic regions—the Appalachian Ridge and Valley, the Highlands, the Piedmont, and the Atlantic Coastal Plain.

Cape May is at the southern tip of the New Jersey coastline.

THE APPALACHIAN RIDGE AND VALLEY

The Appalachian Ridge and Valley is in the northwestern corner of New Jersey. In this region is Kittatinny Ridge, where you'll find the highest elevation in New Jersey—High Point, which stands at 1,803 feet (550 meters). The Kittatinny is part of the Appalachian Mountain range, which stretches from Newfoundland, in Canada, down to Alabama.

Also in this area are the Delaware River and the gorge known as the Delaware Water Gap. The Delaware Water Gap, where the Delaware River has cut through Kittatinny Ridge over millions of years, has rock walls more than 1,000 feet (305 m) high. It is considered one of the most spectacular natural wonders on the East Coast.

Within the Appalachian Ridge and Valley region lies part of the Great Appalachian Valley, which stretches from the Hudson River to Alabama. This area is home to many of New Jersey's dairy farms.

THE HIGHLANDS

About 18,000 years ago, the Wisconsin ice sheet formed glaciers that moved through New Jersey. A glacier is a large mass of ice that moves slowly down mountains and across valleys. These glaciers carved out the hills known as the Highlands (also called the New England Uplands), a region that covers the northern third of New Jersey. They also formed glacial lakes, such as Great Swamp, and the marshy Hackensack Meadowlands.

You can get a good view of the New Jersey landscape from the top of Kittatinny Ridge.

A great blue heron makes itself at home in the Great Swamp.

The Highlands, which begin at the southeastern side of the Appalachian Valley, contain many mountains, hills, and woodlands. Northern New Jersey's dense forests are home to its state tree, the red oak. In spring and summer, buttercups, daisies, Queen Anne's lace, and purple violets—New Jersey's state flower—bloom. Azalea and rhododendron bushes are also native to the Highlands region.

In the late seventeenth century, settlers discovered that the Highlands contained iron ore. Native Americans referred to iron ore as "Succysunny," or "black stone." Iron mining in New Jersey contin-

FIND OUT MORE

Some scientists believe that the Appalachian Mountains were once higher than the Himalayas of Asia, whose peaks rise to nearly 30,000 feet (9,144 m). However, much can happen in hundreds of millions of years, and the highest Appalachian peaks are now just a few thousand feet above sea level. What types of natural occurrences could have worn down the mountains?

ued into the 1960s, along with that of zinc, which was mined from the mid-1800s until 1954, when zinc deposits were exhausted.

THE PIEDMONT

The Piedmont is the strip of New Jersey that extends from the northeastern coast along the Hudson River to the western shores along the Delaware River. Many major rivers flow through the Piedmont, including the Hudson and the Delaware Rivers. The cliffs of the Palisades, a National Historic Landmark formed from volcanic rock, tower 500 feet (152 m) above the Hudson River, across from New York City. Also in this region is Great Falls, a 77-foot (23-m) high waterfall around which the city of Paterson was built.

THE ATLANTIC COASTAL PLAIN

The Wisconsin ice sheet and its glaciers, which formed the mountains, hills, glacial lakes, and waterfalls of northern New Jersey, stopped near what is now Newark, leaving the middle and southern areas of the state untouched. This flatter area is known as the Atlantic Coastal Plain, extending 127 miles (204 km) from Sandy Hook to Cape May Point. The Atlantic Coast in New Jersey, often called the Jersey shore, extends about 130 miles. The Jersey shore is a popular vacation spot on the East Coast. It is lined with resort towns and sandy beaches.

Great Falls is a natural landmark in New Jersey.

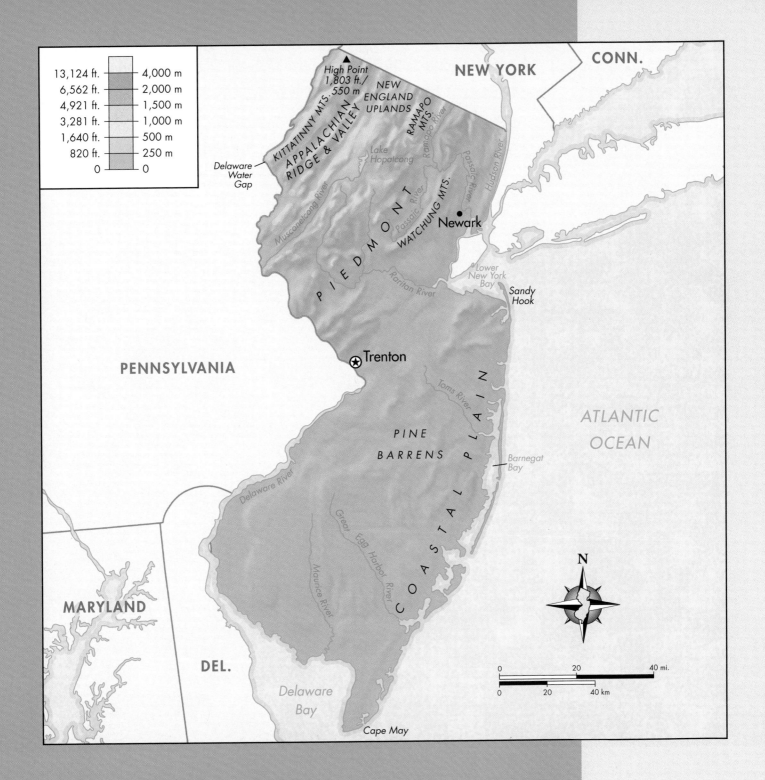

KITTATINNY MTS.

APPALACHIAN RIDGE & VALLEY

NEW ENGLAND UPLANDS

RAMAPO MTS.

▲ High Point
1,803 ft./
550 m

Delaware Water Gap

Lake Hopatcong

Musconetcong River

Ramapo River

Passaic River

Hudson River

PIEDMONT

Passaic River

WATCHUNG MTS.

● Newark

Raritan River

Lower New York Bay

Sandy Hook

⊛ Trenton

Toms River

COASTAL PLAIN

PINE BARRENS

Barnegat Bay

Delaware River

Great Egg Harbor River

Maurice River

PENNSYLVANIA

MARYLAND

DEL.

Delaware Bay

Cape May

NEW YORK

CONN.

ATLANTIC OCEAN

13,124 ft. — 4,000 m
6,562 ft. — 2,000 m
4,921 ft. — 1,500 m
3,281 ft. — 1,000 m
1,640 ft. — 500 m
820 ft. — 250 m
0 — 0

N

0   20   40 mi.
0   20   40 km

A unique geographical area in the Coastal Plain is the Pinelands, or Pine Barrens. The Pinelands is a forest that covers about one-fourth of the southern part of the state. Streams and rivers flow throughout, making it a lush area that contains more than 800 kinds of plants.

Hiking is a good way to explore the dense forests and marshes of the Pine Barrens.

The Pinelands are home to a great variety of wildlife, including the Pine Barrens tree frog. This little creature has been found in only two other places in the world. More than 150 species of birds, flying squirrels, beavers, deer, muskrats, and snakes make their homes there. Close to 100 species of animals and plants in the Pinelands are endangered or threatened. An endangered species is one that is in danger of becoming extinct, and a threatened species is one that is likely to become endangered.

The southwestern corner of the state is the heart of the Garden State's farmland. Agriculture in New Jersey has undergone great changes since Native Americans first planted and harvested crops more than

Thanks to the good soil and climate, New Jersey farms provide food for millions of people.

three centuries ago. Many farms have been sold and the land used to build houses and shopping centers, while some have been turned into parks or nature preserves. However, New Jersey is still home to nearly 10,000 farms.

RIVERS AND LAKES

The Hudson River, on the eastern side of the state, and the Delaware River both originate in New York. The Hudson flows into New York Harbor. The Delaware ends at the Delaware Bay. The Hackensack, Raritan, and Passaic Rivers begin and end within the state.

New Jersey has nearly 400 lakes. Many of New Jersey's lakes have become summer resorts. The largest natural lakes in the state are Lake Hopatcong, Greenwood Lake, Culvers Lake, and Green Pond, which lie in the Piedmont region. Many lakes in New Jersey were artificially made or expanded for recreational use, or to supply water to canals.

CLIMATE

Many New Jerseyans appreciate the fact that winters are not very cold, with temperatures averaging 31°Fahrenheit (−1°Celsius), while its summers are not very hot, with average temperatures around 75°F (24°C). Overall, New Jersey has a mild climate for a northern state. In fact, it is the perfect place for outdoor activities year-round, from swimming in summer to cross-country skiing in winter. The coldest temperature

recorded in New Jersey was −34°F (−37°C) on January 5, 1904, in River Vale. On July 7, 1936, the temperature rose to an all-time high of 110°F (43°C) in Runyon.

Precipitation, or the amount of rain and snowfall in the state, averages 45 inches (114 centimeters) annually. About 50 inches (127 cm) of snow falls each year in the northern mountains, which makes this region great for winter sports such as snowboarding and downhill skiing.

Lake Hopatcong is New Jersey's largest lake. It is a popular spot for boating, fishing, ice skating, and swimming.

Southern New Jersey receives only about 11 inches (28 cm) of snow each year.

New Jersey has experienced droughts, or periods of no rain, as well as severe storms. The summer of 1999 was so dry that many towns did not allow people to water their lawns or fill swimming pools. Then, in September, Hurricane Floyd hit. Floyd dumped record amounts of water on New Jersey. All schools were closed. In some places, such as Bound Brook, people waited on the roofs of their flooded homes to be rescued by boats.

CHAPTER THREE

NEW JERSEY THROUGH HISTORY

About 10,500 B.C., Paleo-Indians were the first people to migrate to the area we now call New Jersey. They came to North America from Siberia, in Russia. Paleo-Indians were nomadic, meaning they traveled from place to place in search of food and water. They hunted large prehistoric animals such as mastodons and wooly mammoths.

By 7,000 B.C. descendants of the Paleo-Indians, called the Archaic culture, lived in the forests. They hunted deer, wolves, and other animals, and gathered plants. By this time, the mastodons and wooly mammoths had died out.

About 3,000 years ago, the Lenni-Lenape came to the New Jersey area. It is believed they arrived there from what is now Canada. Lenapes lived peacefully in groups of twenty-five to thirty. Their homes were wood-framed shelters, called longhouses or wigwams, covered with grass

Atlantic City was a popular vacation spot as early as 1900.

19

To travel by river, the Lenni-Lenape made dugout canoes from hollowed out logs.

or bark. Longhouses were rectangular in shape, and wigwams were round. The women planted beans, corn, and squash, while the men hunted deer, bears, and foxes, and fished during the warm months. The Lenape enjoyed music, dance, and storytelling, which were often part of their religious ceremonies.

DECLINE OF THE LENAPES

Italian navigator Giovanni da Verrazano became the first European to explore New Jersey in 1524. The Lenape did not encounter other Europeans until 1609, when Henry Hudson arrived sailing a Dutch ship called the *Half Moon*.

By the time Henry Hudson arrived in 1609, thousands of Lenni-Lenape were already living in the area that is now New Jersey.

Swedish settlers arrived in 1638, but in 1655 the Dutch forced the Swedes out of the area. The Dutch settlements had ten times as many people as did the Swedish settlements.

Many Dutch settlers made a living by trading with the Lenape. The Lenape were eager to trade beaver furs for European goods such as guns, liquor, iron kettles, glass beads, and blankets. Fur trading was big business between the Dutch settlers and the Native Americans. Beaver fur was valuable in Europe, where it was used to make fashionable coats and hats.

Some Dutchmen also ventured into the area around Kittatinny Mountain, near the Delaware Water Gap, to mine copper. Copper mining became one of New Jersey's first industries.

Because Native Americans were skilled hunters, they could get fur more easily than the European settlers.

Although the Dutch and the Native Americans had a successful trading relationship, it wouldn't last long. Along with their goods, Europeans also brought diseases such as smallpox and measles. The Lenape had no medicine to treat these diseases. As a result, thousands of Lenape died in epidemics, in which entire villages came down with a disease.

As more European settlers arrived, the Lenapes' situation went from bad to worse. The settlers wanted Lenape lands. They tricked the Lenape into signing contracts, or agreements, to give up their land. The Lenape often misunderstood the meaning of these contracts because the settlers lied to them.

In 1762, the government of New Jersey gave the Lenape a tract of land in Burlington County, called Brotherton. Brotherton was an Indian reservation, an area of land set aside by the government for use by Native Americans. However, the conditions on the reservation were poor, and the Lenape were unable to pay for the supplies they needed, such as food, clothing, and tools. In 1801, Brotherton was sold, and the money paid for it was used to move its residents to New York. In 1822, the Brotherton Lenape moved to Green Bay, Michigan, and later to Kansas.

Today, surviving members of the Lenape tribe live in Oklahoma, Kansas, Wisconsin, and in Ontario, Canada. A few small groups of

Native Americans still live in New Jersey. The Nanticoke Lenni-Lenape Indians, whose headquarters are in Bridgeton, teach dancing, drumming, and Indian crafts to people. Rankokus Indian Reservation in Burlington County offers classes and festivals to educate New Jerseyans about Native American history, culture, and crafts.

EUROPEAN SETTLEMENTS

In the same way the Dutch had outnumbered the Swedish, the many English people came to greatly outnumber the Dutch settlers. In 1664, England took possession of Dutch-owned New Netherland (Manhattan and the surrounding areas, including present-day New Jersey), renaming the larger Dutch colony New York. Dutch Governor Peter Stuyvesant surrendered without a fight. The smaller colony was named New Jersey, after the English Isle of Jersey.

New Jersey was given to James, the Duke of York, by his brother, King Charles II of England. The Duke of York then gave the area to his friends, Lord John Berkeley and Sir George Carteret. Their respective areas became known as West Jersey and East Jersey.

Sir George Carteret, former governor of the Isle of Jersey, arrived to claim East Jersey.

West and East Jersey developed in different ways. West Jersey was settled by Quakers, a peaceful religious group who had been persecuted in England. They came to New Jersey so that they could practice their religion freely. The Puritans, another religious group from England, had established parts of East Jersey, including Newark, Piscataway, and Woodbridge.

In other areas of East Jersey, huge estates, or large pieces of land, were set up by wealthy landowners. Landowners used indentured servants

The first Quaker meeting house was built in Burlington, New Jersey.

25

FIND OUT MORE

Quakers opposed slavery, believing that all people were born with equal rights to freedom. Slaveowners were not allowed to worship in Quaker meeting houses. In what ways did Quakers work toward abolishing, or putting an end to, slavery in New Jersey?

and African slaves to work on their estates. Indentured servants were poor people whose trip to the New World was paid for by rich colonists. Free of charge, they worked for the person who brought them. In this way, the indentured servants repaid the person who helped them come to the New World. While they were often treated poorly, indentured servants were free to leave when their period of employment—usually seven years—was fulfilled.

Landowners also used large numbers of African slaves, who were first brought to New Jersey by the Dutch in the mid-1600s. Slaves—men, women, and children alike—were kidnapped by Europeans, brought to the colonies, and sold to landowners like furniture or other property. Slaves worked without pay, and many were not treated well by their owners. Most slaves lived in shacks, and were provided with little food and shabby clothing. They were sometimes beaten if they disobeyed their owners.

A REVOLUTION BEGINS

In 1702, West and East Jersey became united as one colony. In 1738, Lewis Morris was named Royal Governor. As Royal Governor, he ruled New Jersey, but his decisions were subject to the approval of the English government. Over time, many colonists resented being controlled by England. In particular, they were becoming dissatisfied with the taxes, or extra money they were required to pay to the British (English) government for English goods.

Many colonists protested British control by giving dramatic speeches.

Taxes were placed on many everyday goods, including paper products (newspapers and official documents) and sugar. Most colonists felt that, since they were not represented in the English government, the taxes were unfair. Protestors adopted the saying, "no taxation without representation." By the 1770s, the number of Patriots, or anti-British colonists, was growing. Patriots encouraged people in all the colonies, including New Jersey, to support independence from England.

In 1775, the American Revolution, also called the Revolutionary War (1775–1783), broke out between the colonies and England. Because New Jersey was located between the cities of New York and Philadelphia, it became the site of several major Revolutionary War battles. One of the most famous battles took place in Trenton. On Christmas night in 1776, George Washington's army crossed the Delaware River to surprise the Hessians, who were German soldiers hired by the British army. The Hessians had spent Christmas Day eating. They were groggy and unable to defend themselves, and as a result, Washington and his men won the Battle of Trenton in a few short hours. A week later, Washington's army once again defeated the British at Princeton. In 1783, the war ended with the colonies victorious.

On December 18, 1787, New Jersey ratified, or approved, the Constitution of the United States. The Constitution is a document that states the basic laws of the United States, and provides the framework for the way our government is organized. On the same day, New Jersey became the third state of the newly formed United States. Trenton was named the capital in 1790.

Washington led his troops to victory at the Battle of Princeton.

A LAND OF OPPORTUNITY

Winning the American Revolution meant that Americans were now free from having to follow the laws of England. Many Americans felt the United States should start its own industries, or manufacturing businesses, so they would also be less dependent upon English products. To produce goods in New Jersey, it was necessary to build factories and mills. Transportation was also needed to bring supplies to those factories, and to haul away the finished products. Goods were shipped within the state, as well as between New York and Philadelphia, the nation's two most important cities at the time.

The railroad from Camden to Perth Amboy was completed in 1834.

By 1830, about 550 miles (880 km) of new roads had been built in New Jersey, helping industries to transport their goods for sale. Canals were also built to improve transportation. Canals, or man-made waterways, were dug with picks and shovels by thousands of New Jersey workers, many of whom came from Ireland. These canals allowed goods to be transported more inexpensively and quickly than they could along roads.

New Jersey's industries developed with the railroads. New and larger factories were built alongside the railroad lines, which could transport supplies and finished products quickly. Industries that grew with the rail-

A young girl lights the furnace at an iron mill in Boontown.

roads included textiles such as cotton and silk in Paterson, iron in Trenton, bricks and rubber in New Brunswick, and brewing (making beer), in Newark.

The development of industries, including ironmaking, papermaking, and glassblowing, led to a great population increase in New Jersey. Many Europeans saw it as a land of opportunity. They found work in the many factories that produced soap, bricks, pencils, steel, pottery, flour, and textiles.

EXTRA! EXTRA!

John Stevens from Hoboken built the first steam locomotive in the United States. After demonstrating the locomotive on a 600-foot (183-m) circular track in 1825, the government of New Jersey granted Stevens permission to build the Camden and Amboy Railroad. When the line was completed in 1839, the distance between Philadelphia and New York—nearly 100 miles (161 km)—could be traveled in seven hours. In contrast, a trip from New York to Philadelphia along the Delaware & Raritan Canal took nearly two days.

These factories operated in cities such as Newark, Jersey City, Trenton, and Paterson.

Many products manufactured in New Jersey were shipped to southern states. Wealthy landowners bought goods such as fine clothing, jewelry, glassware, and leather saddles. They also bought cheap clothing and shoes for slaves who worked in the South.

THE CIVIL WAR

New Jersey, along with the other northern states, no longer allowed slavery. However, southern states needed workers for their large cotton plantations. They wanted slavery to continue.

Many New Jerseyans felt that each state should have the right to decide for itself whether to abolish slavery or not. New Jersey businessmen knew that if they angered Southerners by speaking out against slavery, the wealthy people of the South would no longer buy their goods. They did not want to risk losing business.

At the same time, Quakers and other New Jerseyans opposed slavery and thought it should be

The home of Elizabeth and Abigail Goodwin in Salem was a famous stop on the Underground Railroad.

stopped. They helped slaves escape from the South on the Underground Railroad. This was not a real railroad, but a secret network of people and places where slaves could hide on their journey to freedom. Many slaves traveled as far north as Canada.

In 1860, Abraham Lincoln was elected president. Lincoln was against slavery, and some southern states feared that he would try to end the practice. In protest, several southern states seceded, or withdrew, from the United States. They banded together and formed a new nation, called the Confederate States of America. It wasn't long before war broke out.

During the Civil War (1861–1865), New Jersey sent troops to fight in the Union Army of the North, though many New Jerseyans supported the South. Eighty-eight thousand soldiers from the state served in the Civil War, and about 6,300 died. The war ended in 1865 with the North victorious.

WHAT'S IN A NAME?

Many names of places in New Jersey have interesting origins.

Name	Comes From or Means
Delaware River	Thomas West, Baron De La Warr, governor of the Virginia colony
Trenton	William Trent, a merchant who developed Trenton in the early 1700s
Hoboken	Lenape word meaning "tobacco pipe" or "land of the tobacco pipe"
Batsto	Native American word meaning "bathing place"
Paterson	William Paterson, New Jersey governor from 1790 to 1793
Hudson River	Henry Hudson, who explored New Jersey in 1609
Elizabeth	Wife of Sir George Carteret, colonial proprietor of East Jersey from 1664 to 1680
Cape May	Dutch explorer Cornelius Jacobson Mey
Passaic	Minsi (Lenape) word for "valley"

As New Jersey entered the late 1800s, it was clearly becoming an urban state. In addition to the Irish, who had come in the earlier part of the century to build canals, the state became the new home of thousands of people from Italy, Russia, Poland, and Czechoslovakia. By the middle of the 1870s, New Jersey had more than one million residents.

The late 1800s were an era of new ideas and progress. In 1876, inventor Thomas Edison set up what he called an "invention factory" in

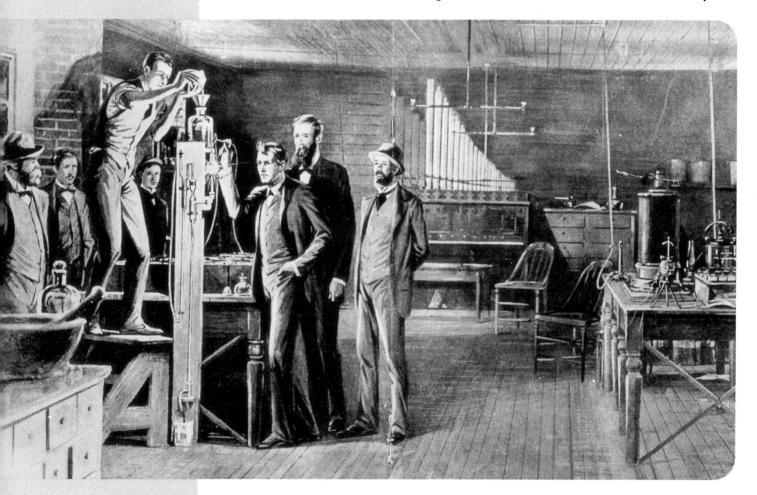

Thomas Edison and his coworkers test a lightbulb at his lab in Menlo Park.

Menlo Park. It was there that Edison developed ideas that would change the way people lived and worked. After he invented the phonograph (an early version of the record player) in 1877, Edison invented the first practical electric lamp (light bulb) and developed the motion picture camera and film. The world's first motion picture studio was built on the grounds of Edison's invention factory in New Jersey.

Industry mixed with agriculture in the early 1900s, when food-processing plants opened. These plants canned and froze vegetables and fruits. Joseph Campbell introduced canned tomato and vegetable soup from his factory in Camden. Campbell's factory grew to become the world-famous Campbell's Soup Company.

WORLD WAR I

In 1917, New Jersey, along with the rest of the United States, joined the Allied forces of England, Russia, and France against Germany in World

Workers at the New York Shipbuilding Corporation in Camden built many ships for the United States Navy.

War I (1914–1917). This war killed more than eight million people.

New Jersey factories turned toward producing supplies for the war. More ships were built in the Hudson River shipyards than were built in any other state. More than 500,000 soldiers sailed for Europe from Hoboken's "port of embarkation."

This increase in factory production required more workers. As fewer immigrants came from Europe, employers looked elsewhere for people to hire. Factory owners encouraged African-Americans from the South to come to New Jersey. Between 1911 and 1917, the African-American population in New Jersey nearly tripled, jumping from about 11,000 to almost 30,000.

Factory owners did not help to provide housing for the African-American workers, however. Many landlords would not rent houses or apartments to African-Americans. Those who did charged very high rents for dirty and undesirable living spaces such as shacks, cellars, and basements.

HARD TIMES

After the war, unemployment rose. People lost their jobs because the production of New Jersey factories was down. Many goods that had been manufactured during wartime, such as ships, ammunition, uniforms, blankets, and tents, were no longer needed.

In 1920, a new amendment, or law, called prohibition was passed in many states, including New Jersey. Prohibition outlawed the drinking or selling of alcoholic beverages. People who supported prohibition felt that alcohol caused people to behave violently, and that the use of liquor contributed to people losing their jobs and neglecting their families.

Despite the laws, many people still wanted liquor. Prohibition resulted in a new underground, or illegal, industry in the state. Many boats illegally brought liquor from Canada and the Caribbean, and the New Jersey shoreline became known as Rum Row (rum is a type of liquor). Members of organized crime gangs hired people to import, transport, and sell illegal liquor. This was known as bootlegging. Prohibition finally ended in 1933. One reason was that many people felt more jobs would become available if the

FAMOUS FIRSTS

- First copper mine in America was at Kittatinny Mountain, 1640
- First practical submarine was built by John Holland in Passaic County, 1878
- First airplane passenger service started in Atlantic City, 1919
- First World Series radio broadcast was in Newark, 1921
- First electric guitar was invented by Les Paul in Mahwah, 1940
- First robot to replace a human worker was used by the General Motors Company in Ewing Township, 1961

sale of liquor was a legal industry. Others believed prohibition did not allow people the right to make decisions for themselves.

The 1920s ended with the stock market crash of 1929. This occurred, in part, because industries had developed quickly and were producing more goods than people could buy. Many people were borrowing money to buy stock, or a small piece of ownership of a company. They believed the stocks would become more valuable over time and could later be sold for a large profit.

On October 29, 1929, known as Black Tuesday, people sold millions of stocks, and the stock market crashed. With everyone selling and no one buying, people and businesses all over the United States lost tremendous amounts of money. Many people lost all the money they had. Businesses had to shut down because they had no money to operate. Also, people had no money to buy the goods produced by the businesses. This caused more than one hundred New Jersey banks to close. Many New Jersey mills and factories also closed. Thousands of people lost their jobs, savings, and homes. This period in history is known as the Great Depression (1929–1939).

In 1933, Franklin D. Roosevelt was elected president. Roosevelt started many work programs, which created more than 100,000 jobs for New Jersey men and women. These people were employed doing public works such as improving parks and building public schools. Gradually, the country recovered from the depression.

It was not until World War II (1939–1945), however, that the economy of the state fully recovered. The United States joined the war

in 1941 to fight against Germany, Italy, and Japan. Once again, factories opened to produce wartime supplies and ammunition. Five hundred thousand new jobs were created in the early 1940s. Many new workers were women, because men were overseas fighting in the war. More than 500,000 New Jerseyans served in World War II, and 13,000 lost their lives.

This photo shows a view of Newark in 1935.

(opposite)
The National Guard patrolled the streets during the Newark riot.

After the war, the population of New Jersey rose and the economy prospered. Suburbs began to develop outside the cities. Many people chose to leave New Jersey cities to move to these suburban areas. When people left, their tax monies no longer contributed to the maintenance of city schools and housing. As a result, the conditions of New Jersey cities began to worsen.

During World War II, more African-Americans moved to New Jersey to work in the industries there. Hispanic people arrived from places such as Puerto Rico. These working-class people lived in cities that were crowded and run down. Eventually, people became angry and frustrated over their living conditions. In 1967, rioting broke out on the streets of Newark. Twenty-six people were killed and 1,500 were injured.

In 1970, Kenneth Gibson was elected mayor of Newark. He tried to improve conditions in the city. The state government also had plans to improve New Jersey's urban areas, but problems continued. Along with people, many businesses moved out of New Jersey cities, and factories closed. This meant fewer jobs for city residents, resulting in more unemployment, and often, more crime.

In 1978, things began to look up. The state government voted to allow legalized gambling in Atlantic City. This created a new industry for the state, which in turn created many new jobs. In the same year, the Meadowlands Sports Complex, which includes a stadium and indoor arena, opened in East Rutherford. The Meadowlands is home

Giants Stadium, home of the New York Giants and the New York Jets, is part of the Meadowlands Sports Complex.

to the New Jersey Nets basketball team, the New Jersey Devils hockey team, and the NFL New York Jets and New York Giants. World Cup women's soccer and men's World Cup soccer semifinals have been held at the Meadowlands. The stadium has hosted many major rock concerts, including the Rolling Stones, U2, and the Grateful Dead.

In addition to providing new jobs, Atlantic City casinos and the Meadowlands pay taxes to the state. The tax money is used to maintain and upgrade roads, buildings, parks, and housing.

However, improving New Jersey required more than just economic help. Years of industry had resulted in New Jersey becoming one of the most polluted states in the country. For decades, factories, mills, and chemical plants dumped waste in the rivers and on the land, without considering the consequences to people or wildlife. By the 1980s and 1990s, the state was in need of environmental help. In the early 1980s, the Environmental Cleanup Act was passed by the state government. Under this law, companies are forced to clean up all toxic or poisonous waste caused by their factories or plants before they close or move out of the area.

In addition, many New Jersey environmental groups are working toward preserving, or protecting, its natural resources. They are also helping to restore populations of the state's endangered species. These groups work to provide safe habitats where the animals can breed. Other programs, such as the National Wildlife Federation's Backyard Wildlife Habitat program, teach people about the importance of preserving habitats for animals and plants that are native to the area.

The environment was still a concern throughout the 1990s. More areas of the state were being developed into housing and shopping centers, resulting in habitat loss for many animals. New Jersey residents in suburban areas complained of deer and bears causing damage to their gardens and property. Many people feel that bear hunting, which has been outlawed in New Jersey since 1970, should now be allowed. This issue is still being discussed by governmental and wildlife groups.

New Jersey's cities saw improvements in the 1990s. In 1997, the New Jersey Performing Arts Center opened in Newark. The center is home to the New Jersey Symphony Orchestra, the New Jersey State Opera, and several theatre and dance companies. It was part of the rebuilding of downtown Newark, along with the opening of the River-front baseball stadium in 1999. Trenton has also taken great steps in bringing new life to its downtown area. The Sovereign Bank Arena, a $53 million sports and entertainment center, opened in 1999, in what was once the American Wire and Steel Factory.

The New Jersey Performing Arts Center attracts many people to downtown Newark.

As New Jersey enters the new millennium, it has great potential to grow and prosper. New Jerseyans are proud of their state. By learning from their past, they will be better able to create a bright future for the people, environment, and industries of the Garden State.

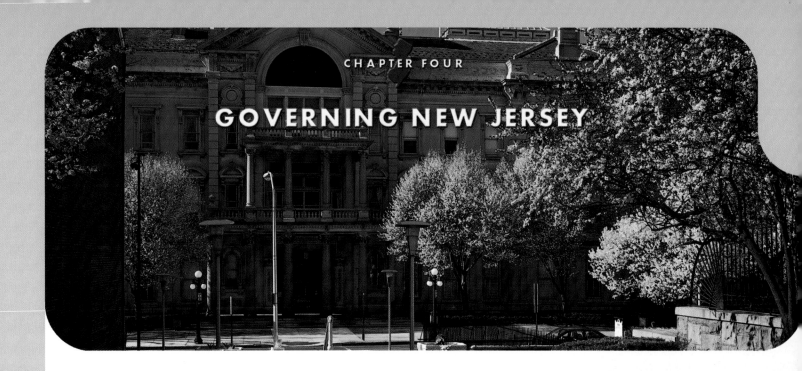

CHAPTER FOUR

GOVERNING NEW JERSEY

New Jersey's laws are established in its state constitution. A constitution is a document that outlines the organization of a state's government, and defines the rights of its citizens. New Jersey has had three constitutions. The original constitution was approved in 1776, and a second in 1844. The current constitution was approved in 1947. Amendments, or changes, require the approval of New Jersey voters in an election. The constitution provides for three branches of government: the executive, the legislative, and the judicial.

New Jerseyans have great respect for their historic capitol building and work hard to preserve it.

EXECUTIVE BRANCH

The executive branch enforces and carries out the laws of New Jersey. This branch is headed by the governor, who is elected by the people.

Other executive officers, including the treasurer, attorney general, and secretary of state, are appointed, or chosen, by the governor.

It is the governor's job to keep the state running smoothly. The governor's responsibilities include making the state budget, or plan for spending of the state's money. He or she also makes decisions in statewide emergencies such as hurricanes or storms. The governor also serves as commander in chief of the state's militia, or armed forces.

LEGISLATIVE BRANCH

The primary job of the legislative branch is to make state laws. The legislature consists of two parts, called houses—the senate and the general assembly. There are 40 senators and 80 members of the general assembly. Senators serve four-year terms, and members of the assembly serve two-year terms.

Bills, or proposed new laws, may be introduced by the assembly or the senate. If a majority of senators and assembly members vote in favor of the bill, it goes to the governor for approval. The governor may approve the bill, signing it into law, or veto the bill, which means to reject it.

JUDICIAL BRANCH

The judicial branch interprets, or explains, the meaning of laws. This responsibility is carried out by the court system. The courts hear cases relating to all kinds of law-related issues, from crimes and accidents to divorces and faulty products.

The judicial branch consists of a number of courts, including the supreme court, the superior court, and the municipal court. Many cases begin in municipal court. Municipal court hears cases involving minor offenses, such as shoplifting, traffic violations, and disputes between people. Six million cases are heard each year in New Jersey municipal courts.

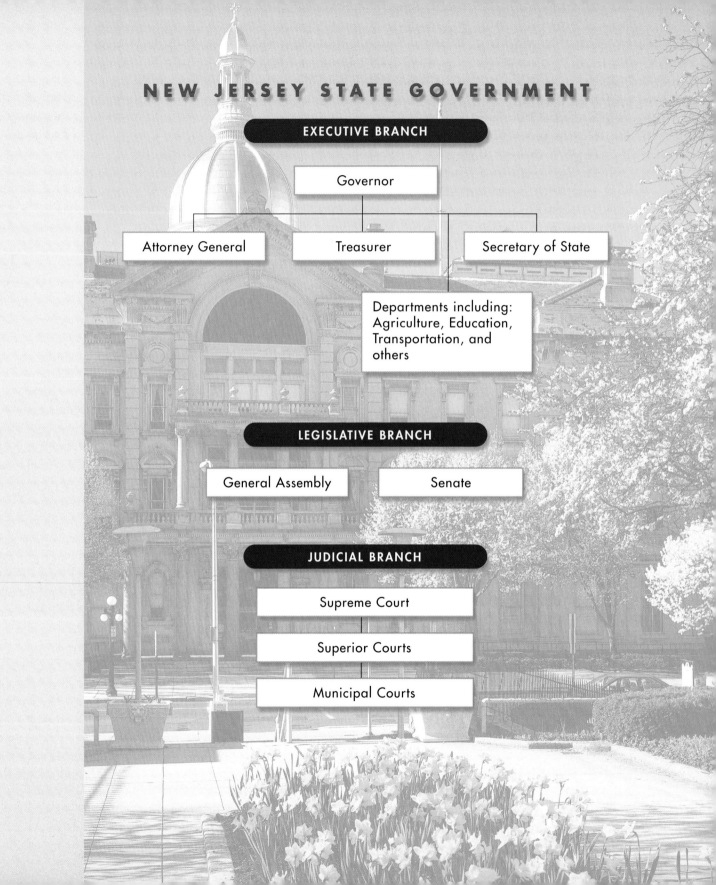

NEW JERSEY STATE GOVERNMENT

EXECUTIVE BRANCH

Governor

Attorney General

Treasurer

Secretary of State

Departments including: Agriculture, Education, Transportation, and others

LEGISLATIVE BRANCH

General Assembly

Senate

JUDICIAL BRANCH

Supreme Court

Superior Courts

Municipal Courts

NEW JERSEY GOVERNORS

Name	Term	Name	Term
William Livingston	1776–1790	Leon Abbett	1890–1893
Elisha Lawrence	1790	George T. Werts	1893–1896
William Paterson	1790–1793	John W. Griggs	1896–1898
Elisha Lawrence	1793	Foster M. Voorhees	1898
Richard Howell	1793–1801	David O. Watkins	1898–1899
Joseph Bloomfield	1801–1802	Foster M. Voorhees	1899–1902
John Lambert	1802–1803	Franklin Murphy	1902–1905
Joseph Bloomfield	1803–1812	Edward C. Stokes	1905–1908
Charles Clark	1812	John Franklin Fort	1908–1911
Aaron Ogden	1812–1813	Woodrow Wilson	1911–1913
William S. Pennington	1813–1815	James F. Fielder	1913
William Kennedy	1815	Leon R. Taylor	1913–1914
Mahlon Dickerson	1815–1817	James F. Fielder	1914–1917
Jesse Upson	1817	Walter E. Edge	1917–1919
Isaac H. Williamson	1817–1829	William N. Runyon	1919–1920
Garret D. Wall	1829	Clarence E. Case	1920
Peter D. Vroom	1829–1832	Edward I. Edwards	1920–1923
Samuel L. Southard	1832–1833	George S. Silzer	1923–1926
Elias P. Seeley	1833	A. Harry Moore	1926–1929
Peter D. Vroom	1833–1836	Morgan F. Larson	1929–1932
Philemon Dickerson	1836–1837	A. Harry Moore	1932–1935
William Pennington	1837–1843	Clifford R. Powell	1935
Daniel Haines	1843–1845	Horace G. Prall	1935
Charles C. Stratton	1845–1848	Harold G. Hoffman	1935–1938
Daniel Haines	1848–1851	A. Harry Moore	1938–1941
George F. Fort	1851–1854	Charles Edison	1941–1944
Rodman M. Price	1854–1857	Walter E. Edge	1944–1947
William A. Newell	1857–1860	Alfred E. Driscoll	1947–1954
Charles S. Olden	1860–1863	Robert B. Meyner	1954–1962
Joel Parker	1863–1866	Richard Hughes	1962–1970
Marcus L. Ward	1866–1869	William T. Cahill	1970–1974
Theodore F. Randolph	1869–1872	Brendan T. Byrne	1974–1982
Joel Parker	1872–1875	Thomas H. Kean	1982–1990
Joseph D. Bedle	1875–1878	James J. Florio	1990–1994
George B. McClellan	1878–1881	Christine Todd Whitman	1994–2001
George C. Ludlow	1881–1884	Donald T. DiFrancesco	2001–2002
Leon Abbett	1884–1887	James E. McGreevey	2002–
Robert S. Green	1887–1890		

If someone does not agree with the decision a court has made, they may appeal their case. The case then goes to a higher court for a new trial. These higher courts are called appellate courts. There are two appellate courts in New Jersey—superior court and the supreme court. Superior court, sometimes called trial court, is where criminal, civil, and family law cases are tried.

The state supreme court is the highest, or most important court in New Jersey. It is made up of seven justices (judges). The governor nominates, or recommends, a person to be a justice, and then the state senate votes on the governor's choice. If selected, a justice serves a seven-year term, after which he or she may be reappointed.

Several old buildings on State Street stand as a reminder of the city's past.

TAKE A TOUR OF TRENTON, THE STATE CAPITAL

Trenton, New Jersey's capital, is located on the western border of the state along the Delaware River. It was named after William Trent, who helped develop the city. Trenton was first settled by Quakers in 1679. In 1790 it was named New Jersey's state capital.

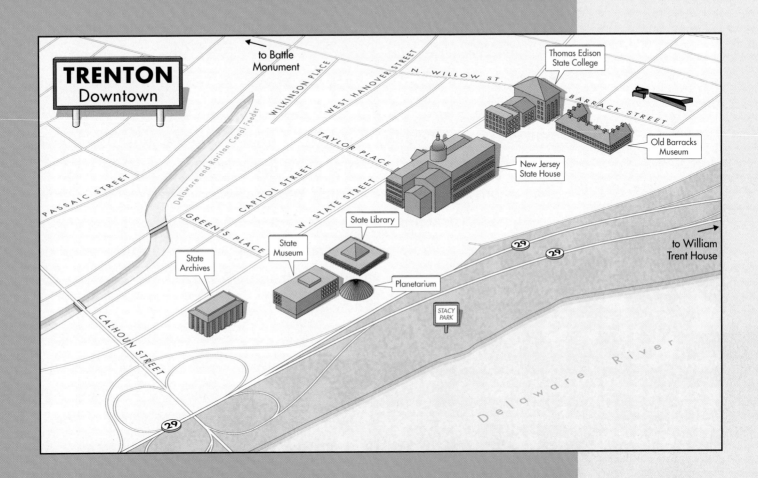

TRENTON
Downtown

to Battle Monument

Thomas Edison State College

N. WILLOW ST.

WEST HANOVER STREET

WILKINSON PLACE

BARRACK STREET

Old Barracks Museum

TAYLOR PLACE

CAPITOL STREET

Delaware and Raritan Canal Feeder

PASSAIC STREET

New Jersey State House

W. STATE STREET

GREEN'S PLACE

State Library

State Museum

State Archives

Planetarium

CALHOUN STREET

29

29

to William Trent House

STACY PARK

29

Delaware River

Trenton was the site of the famous 1776 Battle of Trenton. The city is also well-known for being the site of the first professional basketball game in 1896. Today, Trenton is home to many museums and historical sites, a symphony orchestra, a new sports arena, and great restaurants.

The New Jersey state house was built in 1792, two years after Trenton was named the state capital. On March 21, 1885, a fire broke out in the state house, destroying the roof, the rotunda, the dome, and many offices. The temperature was so cold that the fire-fighting equipment froze. By the time the blaze was put out, major damage had been done. The reconstruction, or rebuilding, of the new capitol was completed in 1889, when the dome was covered with gold leafing. In 1997, New Jersey schoolchildren helped raise money for the restoration, or repair, of the dome. The students raised more than the $48,000 necessary to purchase the 48,000 pieces of new gold leafing.

Within the State House Historic District is the New Jersey State Museum, where you can see Native American artifacts, mastodon skeletons, and a replica of a mine. Then, take a seat in the museum's planetarium to find out more about space exploration and the solar system.

Not far from the capitol is the Old Barracks Museum, built in 1758. There you can visit rooms where some members of George Washington's army ate and slept,

The New Jersey State Museum planetarium has models of the solar system and other astronomy exhibits.

and see the surgeon's office to learn how doctors treated injuries and illness during revolutionary times.

A visit to Trenton wouldn't be complete without a trip to Washington Crossing State Park, where George Washington and his army crossed the Delaware River on Christmas night of 1776. The park is also a popular place for hiking, picnicking, and cross-country skiing in winter.

The William Trent House is said to be Trenton's oldest standing house. It was built in 1719. Trent was a Philadelphia merchant who helped to develop Trenton in the early 1700s. The Trent House was also the home of New Jersey's first colonial governor, Lewis Morris.

Step inside the William Trent house to get an idea of what life was like in colonial times.

THE PEOPLE AND PLACES OF NEW JERSEY

Cape May is well known for Victorian homes such as these.

People from a variety of backgrounds and cultures live in New Jersey. About 7 in every 10 of New Jersey's 8,414,350 residents are of European descent. Italians make up the largest part of this group, but New Jersey's diverse population also includes people of English, Irish, Polish, German, and Russian ancestry.

African-Americans make up about 13 of every 100 people in New Jersey. Some African-Americans can trace their roots back to African slaves three hundred years ago. Others are more recent immigrants or descendants of immigrants from Caribbean islands such as Haiti and Jamaica.

About 13 in every 100 New Jerseyans are of Hispanic descent. They came mainly from Puerto Rico, Cuba, the Dominican Republic, and Central and South America. Asian people from China, Japan, Korea, India, and other areas of the continent comprise almost 6 in every 100 residents. Native Americans make up fewer than 1 in every 100 people. Four hundred years ago, the entire population of New Jersey was Native American.

Three of every four New Jerseyans live in cities. Traveling away from these densely populated urban areas you will find miles of suburbs, lined with houses surrounded by neatly trimmed lawns and fences. Many people in New Jersey choose to live in suburban areas because they are close to the cities, but offer more space, less noise, and safer neighborhoods. If you keep going, you'll see larger tracts of farmland, forests, and wetlands. When you get to the Pinelands, the number of people who live in a square mile area drops to about 10 (compared to more than 900 in the cities). There you really can have more space!

Belleville is a suburb in northern New Jersey.

A Native American dancer in traditional dress performs at the Powhatan Indian Arts festival in Rancocas.

Thanks to the people of New Jersey, just about any type of ethnic food can be found there. If you like Italian food, try Trenton's Italian district, where traditional dishes such as lasagna and calamari (squid), are served. How about sushi (raw fish)? You will find it in the food court at Mitsuwa Marketplace in Edgewater. Japanese, Chinese, and Korean groceries, clothing, books, and other products can also be found at this huge Asian shopping center.

The large Indian-American populations of Edison and Iselin (a community in Woodbridge Township) make these towns good places to go for curry dishes, coconut soup, or delicious Indian breads. You might also see Indian women wearing lovely, colorful saris, or traditional dresses from India.

The Rankokus Indian Reservation in Westampton hosts an art festival, where you will find Native American crafts and food. Visitors can also learn about Native American culture at the Indian Heritage museum in Rancocas.

More than four million people work in New Jersey. Most work in service industries. Service workers provide a service, rather than produce a product. Jobs in this industry include teachers, doctors, government officials, salespeople, and restaurant workers. Banks and insurance companies employ the largest number of service workers in the state. Another growing service industry is tourism, the business of providing shelter, food, and entertainment for visitors. Nearly 800,000 people work in tourism, in vacation spots such as Atlantic City, Jersey shore resorts, and ski areas.

Manufacturing brings in the second largest portion of the state's economy. New Jersey is the country's number-one producer of chemicals, including soap, cosmetics, and medicine. New Jersey has been called "the nation's medicine chest," because it is a leading manufacturer of drugs. Machinery, clothing, and electronics are also produced in the state's factories, as are familiar food items like M&Ms made in Hackettstown, Oreo cookies baked in Fair Lawn, and Lipton tea, which is produced by a company in Englewood Cliffs.

Johnson & Johnson, a major producer of health care products and pharmaceuticals, is headquartered in New Brunswick.

Although only about one in every 100 New Jerseyans earns a living from agriculture, many farm products are grown in New Jersey. Nursery/greenhouse products are the largest part of the New Jersey agriculture industry. Cranberries, blueberries, peaches, bell peppers, corn, tomatoes, and asparagus are some of the fruits and vegetables grown on New Jersey farms. Dairy and horse farms also contribute to the state's economy. Smaller numbers of people in New Jersey work in the state's fishing, forestry, and mining industries.

Most of New Jersey's blueberries are grown in Atlantic and Burlington counties.

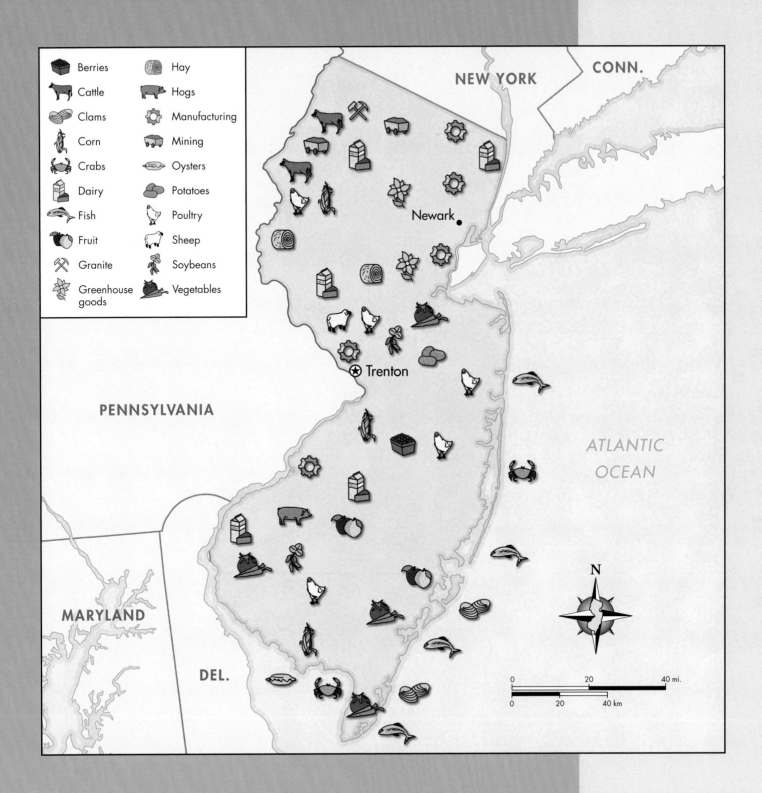

	Berries		Hay
	Cattle		Hogs
	Clams		Manufacturing
	Corn		Mining
	Crabs		Oysters
	Dairy		Potatoes
	Fish		Poultry
	Fruit		Sheep
	Granite		Soybeans
	Greenhouse goods		Vegetables

NEW YORK

CONN.

Newark.

PENNSYLVANIA

ATLANTIC OCEAN

⭐ Trenton

MARYLAND

DEL.

N

0	20		40 mi.
0	20	40 km	

New Jersey is the number-one blueberry-producing state in the country. When they are in season, juicy, delicious blueberries can be found at farmer's markets throughout New Jersey. Remember to ask an adult for help on the recipe below.

NEW JERSEY HARVEST BLUEBERRY MUFFINS

(makes 12 large muffins)
2 cups flour
2/3 cup sugar
2 1/2 teaspoons baking powder
1/4 teaspoon baking soda
1/2 teaspoon salt
1/2 cup butter, melted
2 eggs
1 cup fresh blueberries
1 cup milk

1. Preheat oven to 400°F.
2. Grease muffin pan.
3. In medium bowl, combine dry ingredients.
4. In large bowl, whisk together milk, melted butter, and eggs.
5. Add dry ingredients to liquid mixture.
6. Carefully fold in blueberries.
7. Fill muffin pans about 2/3 full.
8. Bake for 15 to 20 minutes, or until golden brown.
9. Cool in pans for five minutes; remove and cool on wire rack.

TAKE A TOUR OF NEW JERSEY

New Jersey is packed with exciting places and things to do throughout the year. From the mountains to the beaches, fun and excitement await you.

Northern New Jersey

If you love skiing or snowboarding, one of the East Coast's largest ski resorts, Mountain Creek, is in Sussex County in northwestern New Jersey. In summer, Sussex offers lakeside resorts where you can boat, water-ski, swim, or just relax.

One of the most beautiful outdoor places in northern New Jersey is the Delaware Water Gap. Its beautiful mountains, majestic waterfalls, and scenic views of the Delaware River make this visit worth the trip.

More than 4 million visitors enjoy the breathtaking beauty of Delaware Water Gap National Recreation Area each year.

Waterloo Village is a restored historic site that is open to the public.

Many people enjoy hiking, picnicking, and canoeing there. Don't forget to look around for native wildlife such as deer, bears, and bald eagles.

To take in some history, visit Waterloo Village in Stanhope, originally settled in the 1750s. You can see how pottery was crafted, how grain was ground into flour in a grist mill, or how horseshoes were made in the blacksmith shop. You can also experience the Lenape way of life at Waterloo's Lenape Village. This re-creation of a 1625 village includes longhouses and wigwams made of wood and bark, as well as an area like one the European settlers might have visited to trade iron tools, glass, and beads for Lenape animal skins and fur.

As you travel east, stop by Morristown National Historic Park, where the Continental Army endured the brutal winter of 1779–1780. Washington's military headquarters, as well as the Wick House and Farm, home of Tempe Wick, are located within the park. Legend says that Tempe Wick hid her horse in her bedroom for three weeks to protect it from being taken by soldiers during the American Revolution.

Other places of interest include the Morris Museum of Arts and Sciences, and Fosterfields, a working farm dating back to the 1800s. Fosterfields offers tours of the Willows, a mansion on the grounds of the farm. You can learn how butter was churned, how cider was pressed, and how sheep were sheared.

Continue east, and you will reach West Orange, home of the Edison National Historic Site. Further south, in Middlesex County, are the Thomas Edison Memorial Tower and Museum. They are preserved in Menlo Park, where Edison invented the phonograph and worked on the electric light bulb. At the park you can learn about what happened in each building at Edison's laboratory.

Heading toward New York City, stop by Liberty State Park in Jersey City. Liberty Science Center is a museum with three floors of interactive exhibits exploring the environment, health, and inventions. There is a great view of the Statue of Liberty and the New York skyline from Liberty State Park.

WHO'S WHO IN NEW JERSEY?

Edwin "Buzz" Aldrin (1930–) became famous as the second person to walk on the moon. He was also the third person to "walk" in space outside his spacecraft, in 1966. Aldrin was born in Montclair.

From Liberty State Park you can take a ferry to the Statue of Liberty. A replica of Henry Hudson's ship, *The Half Moon*, is docked in the foreground.

Central New Jersey

Next, let's head south to central New Jersey, home of two very old and prestigious universities. At Rutgers University in New Brunswick, the Rutgers University Geology Museum houses the skeleton of a mastodon, an Egyptian mummy, Native American artifacts, fossils, and minerals.

Princeton University was established in 1746. In addition to the university campus, the town of Princeton has many historical sites. Drumthwacket, the official residence of the governor of New Jersey, was built at Princeton in 1835.

Princeton University, once known as the College of New Jersey, was the fourth college to be established in the United States in 1747.

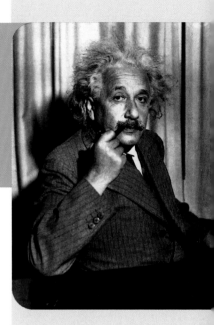

Further south, in Camden, the New Jersey State Aquarium is home to more than 1,400 sea creatures. You can learn about seals at the Seal Shores exhibit, or touch a shark or a stingray at the aquarium's Shark Zone.

Coastal and Southern New Jersey

If the aquarium inspires you to learn more about aquatic life (life in or near the water), head to the shore. The towns along the Atlantic coast offer many opportunities to explore ocean life, as well as wetlands along the shore.

An unusual animal in the town of Margate is Lucy, the 65-foot (20-m) tall, 90-ton (91-metric ton) Margate Elephant. The structure was built in 1881 as an advertisement for a real estate developer. Lucy once served as a hotel, and later as a tavern. Today you can climb the stairs inside Lucy's hind legs to reach a museum inside her belly, and then to an observation deck on her back.

The most popular resort in New Jersey is Atlantic City. This city is famous for its gambling casinos. The world's first boardwalk, a wooden

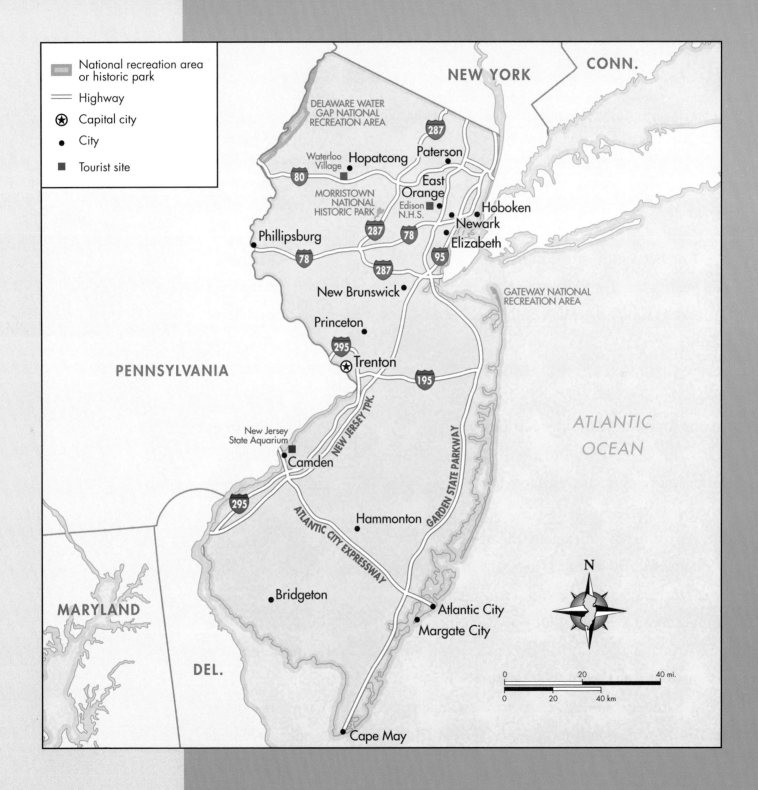

National recreation area or historic park
Highway
⊛ **Capital city**
• **City**
■ **Tourist site**

NEW YORK

CONN.

DELAWARE WATER GAP NATIONAL RECREATION AREA

287

Waterloo Village

Hopatcong

Paterson

80

MORRISTOWN NATIONAL HISTORIC PARK

East Orange

Edison N.H.S.

Hoboken

Phillipsburg

287

287

78

Newark

Elizabeth

95

78

287

New Brunswick

GATEWAY NATIONAL RECREATION AREA

Princeton

295

Trenton

PENNSYLVANIA

195

NEW JERSEY TPK.

ATLANTIC OCEAN

New Jersey State Aquarium

Camden

GARDEN STATE PARKWAY

295

ATLANTIC CITY EXPRESSWAY

Hammonton

MARYLAND

Bridgeton

Atlantic City

Margate City

N

DEL.

0   20   40 mi.

0   20   40 km

Cape May

66

walkway alongside the beach, was built there in 1870. Atlantic City is also home to the Miss America pageant, which has been held there since 1929.

Other popular shore spots are Wildwood and Ocean City, whose great amusement piers make them family favorites. At Island Beach State Park, you can swim and explore nature. At Long Beach Island,

More than thirty million people visit Atlantic City every year.

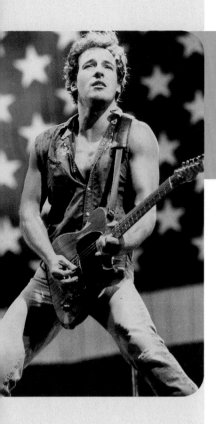

WHO'S WHO IN NEW JERSEY?

Bruce Springsteen (1949–) was one of the most popular rock stars of the 1970s and 1980s. Many of his songs were inspired by his experiences growing up in the Jersey shore area. Springsteen was born in Freehold.

you can see the Barnegat Lighthouse or go on a whale watch. At the southern tip of the state is Cape May, the oldest seaside resort in the United States. Cape May is famous for its beautiful Victorian homes, built in the 1800s. It is also one of the top bird-watching spots in North America.

Inland in southern New Jersey are the Pinelands. At Batsto Village you can learn about life in the Pinelands during the 1800s by touring a water-powered wood mill, a store, a post office, and stables. At Wheaton Village in Millville, find out about the history of glassmaking at the Museum of American Glass. You can see glassware exhibits, as well as demonstrations of glassblowing.

Keep an eye out for the famous Jersey Devil. It is said to have the head of a dog, the face and hooves of a horse, the curled horns of a ram, and the wings of a bat. The story of this creature is that it was born in the Pinelands, or Pine Barrens, as the thirteenth child of a woman named Mother Leeds in 1735. Then the baby turned from a human into a monster. Over the years, many people have reported seeing the New Jersey Devil. Droughts, crop failures, and unexplained deaths have all been blamed on the legendary monster.

New Jersey, small as it is, has made tremendous contributions to the United States. It has been the home of many great people, and the place of many "firsts." It is remarkable that in its tiny area the Garden State offers everything from skiing to swimming, the Statue of Liberty to the Delaware Water Gap, and art museums to professional sports events. New Jerseyans are proud of the hard work and creativity that have helped their state grow into an important place.

Around every corner, New Jersey holds another surprise.

NEW JERSEY ALMANAC

Statehood date and number: December 18, 1787/3rd

State seal: Shows Liberty and Ceres, and a shield with three plows honoring New Jersey's agricultural tradition. The redesigned seal was adopted in 1928.

State flag: The state flag shows the state seal against a gold background. Adopted in 1896.

Geographic center: Plumsted Township, 5 miles (8 km) southeast of Trenton

Total area/rank: 8,204 square miles (21,248 sq km)/47th

Coastline/rank: 130 miles (209 km)/13th

Borders: New York, Delaware bay, Pennsylvania, and the Atlantic Ocean

Latitude and longitude: Approximately 40° N and 75° W

Highest/lowest elevation: 1,801 feet (549 m) at High Point/sea level along the Atlantic shore

Hottest/coldest temperature: 110°F (43°C) at Runyon on July 10, 1936/–34°F (–37°C) at River Vale on January 5, 1904

Land area/rank: 7,419 square miles (19,215 sq km)/46th

Inland water area: 315 square miles

Population (2000 census)/rank: 8,414,350/9th

Population of major cities:

Newark: 273,546

Jersey City: 240,055

Paterson: 149,222

Elizabeth: 120,568

Edison: 97,687

Trenton: 85,403

Camden: 79,904

Origin of state name: Named for the English Channel Isle of Jersey

State capital: Trenton

Counties: 21

State government: 40 senators, 80 assembly members

Major rivers and lakes: Hackensack River, Raritan River, Delaware River, Hudson River, Passaic River, Great Egg Harbor River, Toms River, and Mullica

River; Lake Hopatcong, Lake Mohawk, Greenwood Lake, Budd Lake, Culver Lake, Swartswood Lake, Lake Sunfish, and Green Pond

Farm products: Nursery and greenhouse crops, tomatoes, blueberries, peaches, peppers, cranberries, and potatoes

Livestock: Poultry, cattle, goats, sheep, and horses

Manufactured products: Chemicals, electronic equipment, and food

Mining products: Crushed stone, sand, and gravel

Fishing products: Clams, flounder, sea bass, whiting, crabs, and oysters

Animal: Horse

Bird: Eastern goldfinch

Colors: Blue and buff

Demon: Jersey Devil

Dinosaur: Hadrosaurus

Fish: Brook trout

Flower: Common meadow violet

Folk Dance: Square dance

Insect: Honeybee

Motto: "Liberty and Prosperity"

Nickname: The Garden State

Shell: Knobbed whelk

Tree: Red oak

Wildlife: Red foxes, deer, black bears, raccoons, skunks, chipmunks, possums, hawks, bottlenose dolphins, humpback whales, cottontail rabbits, otters, muskrats, and eastern bobcats

TIMELINE

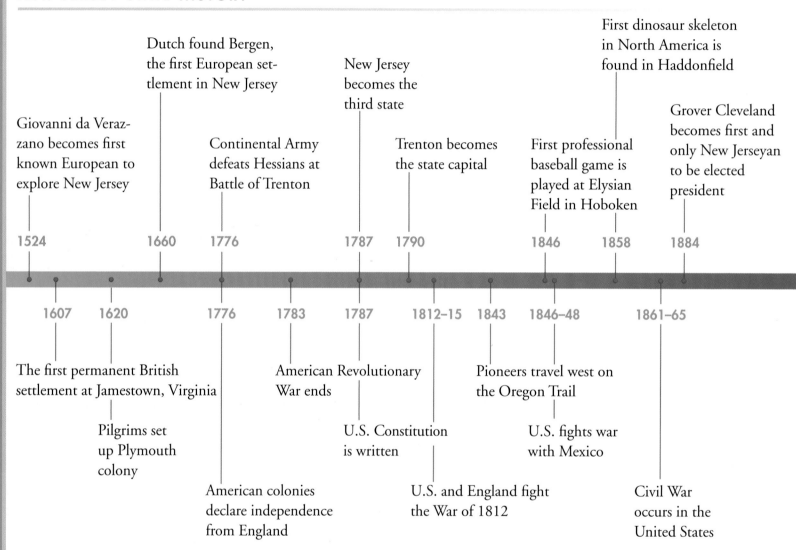

First dinosaur skeleton
in North America is
found in Haddonfield

Dutch found Bergen,
the first European set-
tlement in New Jersey

New Jersey
becomes the
third state

Grover Cleveland
becomes first and
only New Jerseyan
to be elected
president

Giovanni da Veraz-
zano becomes first
known European to
explore New Jersey

Continental Army
defeats Hessians at
Battle of Trenton

Trenton becomes
the state capital

First professional
baseball game is
played at Elysian
Field in Hoboken

1524   1660   1776   1787   1790   1846   1858   1884

1607   1620   1776   1783   1787   1812–15   1843   1846–48   1861–65

The first permanent British
settlement at Jamestown, Virginia

American Revolutionary
War ends

Pioneers travel west on
the Oregon Trail

Pilgrims set
up Plymouth
colony

U.S. Constitution
is written

U.S. fights war
with Mexico

American colonies
declare independence
from England

U.S. and England fight
the War of 1812

Civil War
occurs in the
United States

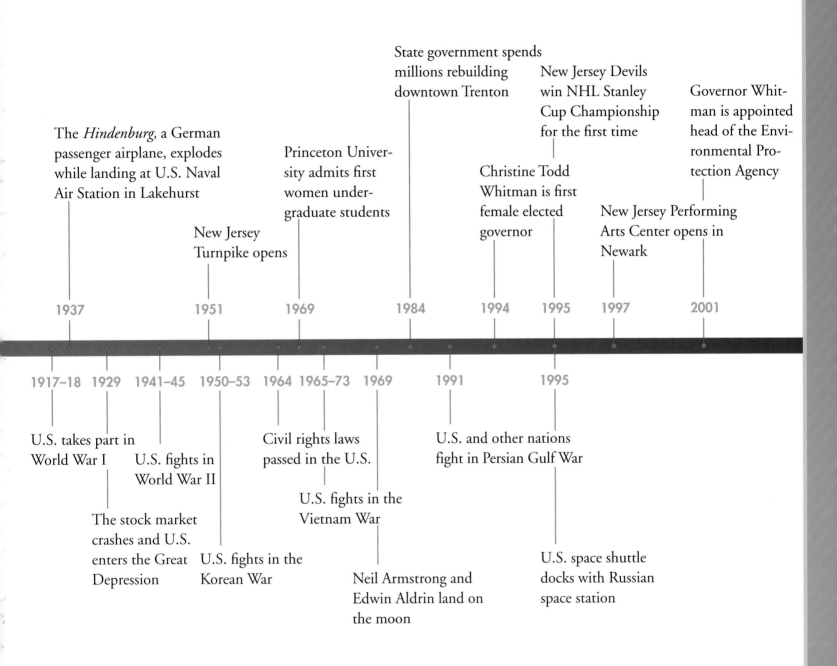

State government spends millions rebuilding downtown Trenton

New Jersey Devils win NHL Stanley Cup Championship for the first time

Governor Whitman is appointed head of the Environmental Protection Agency

The *Hindenburg,* a German passenger airplane, explodes while landing at U.S. Naval Air Station in Lakehurst

Princeton University admits first women undergraduate students

Christine Todd Whitman is first female elected governor

New Jersey Performing Arts Center opens in Newark

New Jersey Turnpike opens

1937   1951   1969   1984   1994   1995   1997   2001

1917–18 1929 1941–45 1950–53 1964 1965–73 1969   1991   1995

U.S. takes part in World War I

U.S. fights in World War II

Civil rights laws passed in the U.S.

U.S. and other nations fight in Persian Gulf War

The stock market crashes and U.S. enters the Great Depression

U.S. fights in the Korean War

U.S. fights in the Vietnam War

Neil Armstrong and Edwin Aldrin land on the moon

U.S. space shuttle docks with Russian space station

GALLERY OF FAMOUS NEW JERSEYANS

Amiri Baraka

(1934–)

Poet and playwright who has written about the struggle of African-Americans. Born in Newark.

William "Count" Basie

(1904–1984)

Famous jazz pianist and composer of the swing era. Born in Red Bank.

Yogi Berra

(1925–)

Professional baseball player for the New York Yankees; manager for the New York Yankees and the New York Mets. He founded the Yogi Berra Museum in Montclair. Lives in Montclair.

Judy Blume

(1938–   )

Author of many well-loved children's books, including *Tales of a Fourth Grade Nothing; Are You There, God? It's Me, Margaret;* and *Tiger Eyes.* Born in Elizabeth.

Grover Cleveland

(1837–1908)

First and only native New Jerseyan to become president of the United States; also the only president elected to two nonconsecutive terms (1885–1889 and 1893–1897). Born in Caldwell.

Alice Paul

(1885–1977)

Founder of the National Women's Party, a group that was organized to fight for women's right to vote. This group introduced the Equal Rights Amendment to the Constitution, written in 1923. Born in Moorestown.

John Travolta

(1954–)

Popular film and television actor. Born in Englewood.

Walt Whitman

(1819–1892)

Poet and journalist; most famous for his collection of poetry entitled *Leaves of Grass.* Lived in Camden.

Woodrow Wilson

(1856–1924)

United States president (1913–1921), New Jersey governor (1911–1913), and president of Princeton University.

Patience Lovell Wright

(1725–1786)

First American sculptor to become internationally known for her wax sculptures. Born in Bordentown.

GLOSSARY

bootlegging: to manufacture, sell, or transport illegally

canal: an artificial waterway

casino: a place where people gamble

consecutive: following in regular or unbroken order; repeated

drought: a long period of dryness that may cause damage to crops

epidemic: outbreak of a disease affecting a large number of people within a population at the same time

erosion: the wearing away of land over time by the action of water, wind, or glacial ice

extinct: died out, no longer existing

glacier: a large body of ice spreading outward on a land surface

Hessians: German soldiers hired by the British army during the Revolutionary War

immigrant: a person who moves from one country to another and lives there permanently

justice: judge

militia: a group of citizens organized for military service

navigator: one who orders and records a ship's course

nomadic: roaming around from place to place

persecution: the act of causing people to suffer because of their beliefs

prehistoric: ancient times, before there were written records

revolution: the overthrow of an established government

urban: relating to a city or town

FOR MORE INFORMATION

Web sites

Lenape (Delaware) Tribe of Indians
http://www.delawaretribeofindians.nsn.us/
Provides information about the history and traditions of the Lenape.

New Jersey History Links
http://www.nj.com/pari/njlinks/index.htm
More than 100 links to New Jersey historical content.

State of New Jersey Web Site
http://www.state.nj.us
Official web site for the State of New Jersey.

State of New Jersey Web Site for Kids
http://www.state.nj.us/hangout
Information about New Jersey for kids.

Books

Cousins, Margaret. *The Story of Thomas Alva Edison.* New York, NY: Random House, 1993.

Sakurai, Gail. *The Thirteen Colonies.* Danbury, CT: Children's Press, 2000.

Schraff, Anne. *Woodrow Wilson (United States Presidents).* Berkeley Heights, NJ: Enslow, 1998.

Addresses

New Jersey Department of Commerce and Economic Development
Division of Travel and Tourism
P. O. Box 826
Trenton, NJ 08625-0826

New Jersey Historical Society
52 Park Place
Newark, NJ 07102

Rankokus American Indian Reservation
P. O. Box 225
Rancocas, NJ 08073

Governor of New Jersey
P. O. Box 001
Trenton, NJ 08625

INDEX

ABOUT THE AUTHOR

Elizabeth Scholl grew up in New York City. As a child, her view of New Jersey was from a car window while traveling on the New Jersey Turnpike.

She received a Bachelor of Arts degree in literature from the State University of New York at Oneonta, and a master's degree in early childhood and elementary education from New York University. She has worked as a teacher and administrator in New York and New Jersey schools, and is currently a freelance writer of educational materials. She writes a column called *Ask the Teacher,* which focuses on school-related issues.

To find out about New Jersey, Elizabeth spent time hiking, vacationing, observing wildlife, and visiting historical sites and museums in the state. She enjoys exploring New Jersey with her husband Fred, and her children, Ethan, Phoebe, and Forrest, as well as spending time with her family at home in Hillsdale.